All you need to know about Costa Rica

Copyright © 2023 Jonas Hoffmann-Schmidt.
Translation: Linda Amber Chambers.

All rights reserved. This book, including all its parts, is protected by copyright. Any use outside the narrow limits of copyright law is prohibited without the written consent of the author. This book has been created using artificial intelligence to provide unique and informative content.

Disclaimer: This book is for entertainment purposes only. The information, facts and views contained therein have been researched and compiled to the best of our knowledge and belief. Nevertheless, the author and the publisher assume no liability for the accuracy or completeness of the information. Readers should consult with professionals before making any decisions based on this information. Use of this book is the responsibility of the reader.

Introduction to Costa Rica: A Land of Wonders 6

The Geography of Costa Rica: Between Coasts and Mountains 9

Discovery of prehistory and early history 12

The Colonial Period: Influence and Legacy 14

Independence and the Emergence of the Republic 17

Modern History: Progress and Political Development 19

The rich diversity of fauna and flora 22

Conservation in Costa Rica: A Pioneer in Environmental Protection 24

From coffee plantations to sustainable agriculture 27

The variety of delicious Costa Rican cuisine 29

The magic of traditional dishes 31

Exotic fruits and their meaning 33

The fascinating wildlife of Costa Rica 36

Rainforest Adventure: On the Trail of Wild Animals 39

Explore the spectacular variety of birds 42

The Majestic Marine Life: Underwater Paradises 45

In the footsteps of indigenous cultures 47

Handicrafts and folk art 50

Religion and Spirituality in Costa Rica 53

Traditional festivals and celebrations 56

San José: The Vibrant Capital 59

Cartago: Historical heritage and modern dynamism 62

The colorful coastal town of Puerto Limón 65

Pura Vida in Puntarenas: beaches and more 68

The historical significance of Heredia 71

Alajuela: Home of the Arenal Volcano 73

Cultural diversity of the population 76

Music and dance: rhythm in the life of the Ticos 79

Literature and Art Scene in Costa Rica 82

Family structures and social norms 85

Education system and intellectual heritage 87

Language and dialects of indigenous peoples 90

The Importance of Ecotourism in Costa Rica 93

National Parks and Protected Areas: Preserving Natural Treasures 96

Beaches, Volcanoes and Adventure: Tourism Highlights 99

The mysterious cloud forest region of Monteverde 102

Manuel Antonio: Tropical beauty and biodiversity 104

The fascinating experience of volcanoes 107

The Future of Costa Rica: Challenges and Opportunities 109

Epilogue 112

Introduction to Costa Rica: A Land of Wonders

Costa Rica, the small country in Central America, is a fascinating paradise that delights visitors with its rich diversity of nature, culture and history. Between the picturesque coasts of the Pacific Ocean and the Caribbean Sea stretches a landscape characterized by majestic volcanoes, dense rainforests, breathtaking beaches and lush lowlands. With an area of only 51,100 square kilometers, Costa Rica may be small, but its importance and uniqueness are enormous.

The country's geography is a fascinating interplay of diverse ecosystems. From the active Arenal Volcano towering majestically into the sky to the misty heights of the Monteverde Cloud Forest, home to an abundance of plants and animals, Costa Rica offers an impressive range of landscapes. But it's not just the natural beauties that make Costa Rica stand out. The country has also made a name for itself as a pioneer in environmental protection and sustainable development. As early as the 1980s, Costa Rica declared a large part of its area as protected areas and national parks, helping to preserve its unique biodiversity.

The history of Costa Rica is as multifaceted as its landscape. From the early indigenous cultures that once inhabited the country to the Spanish colonial era and subsequent independence, Costa Rica has a rich past. The importance of democracy and peace is reflected in the fact that Costa Rica has not had an army for over 70 years. This political model has helped to make the country a stable and peaceful place.

Costa Rica's wildlife is another highlight that attracts nature enthusiasts from all over the world. In the country's rainforests and national parks, visitors can see exotic animals such as monkeys, sloths, jaguars, and colorful birds in their natural environment. The biodiversity is astonishing and contributes to the global conservation of biodiversity.

Costa Rica's culture is characterized by a mix of indigenous traditions, Spanish heritage, and modern influence. Music and dance are integral parts of daily life, and traditional festivals such as the "Dia de la Independencia" reflect people's pride and identity. The friendly and warm nature of Costa Ricans, known as "Ticos", greets visitors with the characteristic expression "Pura Vida", which embodies the positive philosophy of life of the country.

In this book, we will explore the different facets of Costa Rica, from its rich history, to its diverse wildlife, to its cultural treasures and stunning nature. Immerse yourself in the wonders of this unique country and discover why Costa Rica has become an unforgettable destination for adventurers, nature lovers, and culture vultures.

The Geography of Costa Rica: Between Coasts and Mountains

Costa Rica, with its extraordinary geographical diversity, is a true natural paradise in Central America. The country's landscape is characterized by an impressive mix of stunning coastlines, majestic mountains, lush lowlands and dense rainforests. This diversity reflects not only the geological history of the country, but also its climatic range and the resulting biodiversity.

Costa Rica's coastline stretches for about 1,290 kilometers, with the country bordering both the Pacific Ocean and the Caribbean Sea. The Pacific coast is home to endless beaches of sandy splendor, from the lively seaside resorts of Guanacaste to the quieter hideaways of the Nicoya Peninsula. The Caribbean coast, on the other hand, is lined with dense rainforest and tropical vegetation, while colorful coral reefs and turquoise waters make the Caribbean a paradise for divers and snorkelers.

The geographical highlight of Costa Rica is undoubtedly the majestic volcanoes that grace the country. One of the most famous is the Arenal Volcano, which provides an impressive backdrop and is a popular destination for adventure seekers. The Poás volcano, on the other hand, impresses with one of the largest active craters in the world, surrounded by a lush, green environment. The mountain ranges of Costa Rica, such as the Cordillera Central and the Cordillera de Talamanca, offer not only stunning scenery but also a habitat for a rich variety of flora and fauna.

The lowlands of Costa Rica, also known as the "Central Valley," are home to some of the country's most important cities, including the capital, San José. This fertile region is characterized by coffee plantations, flower fields and farms. The distinctive topography of the Central Valley has also led to climatic differences, with different elevations exhibiting different patterns of temperature and precipitation.

Costa Rica's rainforests, which cover about a quarter of the country's land area, are characterized by lush vegetation, exotic plants, and impressive wildlife. The Monteverde Cloud Forest, famous for its suspension bridges and numerous species of birds, as well as Corcovado National Park, considered one of the most biodiverse places on earth, are just a few examples of the fascinating ecosystems that can be found in Costa Rica's rainforests.

The geographical diversity of Costa Rica is a constant source of wonder and inspiration. From the coastal regions to the peaks of the volcanoes, the country offers a variety of landscapes that are not only visually impressive, but also offer a unique insight into the geological and biological history of this extraordinary place.

Discovery of prehistory and early history

The discovery of Costa Rica's prehistory and early history gives us a fascinating look at the long and varied history of this country. The traces of human habitation date back to the time before the arrival of European explorers. Archaeological finds and investigations have made it possible to reconstruct the history of the indigenous peoples who once inhabited the region.

Millennia ago, Costa Rica was home to various indigenous cultures, including the Chorotega, Huetar, Bribri, and Boruca. These peoples created impressive artifacts, including pottery, stone tools, and jewelry, that reflected not only their craftsmanship but also their cultural identity. Many of these artifacts can be found in archaeological sites across the country, such as Guayabo, one of the oldest known sites, estimated to be around 3,000 years old.

The idea of the world and the universe was of great importance to these indigenous cultures. The burial mounds, known as the "chiriquí" style, bear witness to complex burial rituals and the belief in a spiritual connection between the living and the ancestors. The stone balls of

Diquís are another example of cultural significance, as they may have been used for ritual games.

The arrival of Europeans in the 16th century marked a turning point in Costa Rica's history. The Spaniards, led by Christopher Columbus, set foot on the country's shores, bringing with them both cultural influences and diseases that wreaked havoc on the indigenous population. While many indigenous traditions were lost through contact with the Spaniards, some customs and rituals have survived to this day and shape the country's culture.

The discovery of Costa Rica's prehistory and early history is an ongoing process that continues to progress through archaeological research and discoveries. The discoveries in recent decades have deepened our understanding of the way of life, art and culture of indigenous peoples. These insights help us appreciate the rich cultural diversity that has shaped and continues to shape Costa Rica.

The traces of the past are visible everywhere in Costa Rica, whether in the archaeological sites, the remains of ancient settlements, or the stories that have been passed down from generation to generation. The discovery of prehistory and early history reminds us of how deeply rooted the history of the country is and how important it is to preserve and protect this history.

The Colonial Period: Influence and Legacy

Costa Rica's colonial period, which spanned centuries, left a lasting mark on the country, leaving a legacy that is recognizable in the structures, culture, and identity of today's society. The influence of the European colonial powers, especially Spain, left traces that are still visible today in architecture, religion, society and art.

The arrival of the Spanish in the early 16th century led to the conquest and colonization of Costa Rica. The Spaniards brought with them not only their language and religious beliefs, but also new plants, animals and technologies that changed the lives of indigenous peoples. The impact of this cultural encounter was complex and led to the fusion of indigenous traditions with Spanish influences.

During the colonial period, Costa Rica became part of the Viceroyalty of Peru, later part of the Viceroyalty of New Granada, and finally the Viceroyalty of New Spain. However, due to its remote location and relative poverty, Costa Rica had experienced less direct interference from colonial powers than other parts of Latin America. This relative isolation led to society in Costa Rica acting more independently and developing a special identity.

It was during this period that agriculture began to develop, especially the cultivation of coffee, which would later become one of the country's main exports. The colonial rulers established coffee plantations and used the fertile soils to generate economic prosperity. This phase laid the foundation for Costa Rica's role as an exporter of agricultural products.

Colonial-era architecture is reflected in Costa Rica's historic cities. The city of Cartago, once the country's capital, is home to impressive examples of colonial architecture, including the Basilica of Nuestra Señora de los Ángeles, an important religious site. The city of Heredia also bears witness to this era, with its cobbled streets and colonial buildings.

Religion played a central role during the colonial era and had a lasting impact on Costa Rican culture and society. Catholicism was introduced by the Spanish and remained a dominant force influencing people's daily lives. Religious festivals, processions and customs were integrated into the culture and have remained alive to this day.

The colonial era left a legacy deeply rooted in Costa Rica's identity. The blend of indigenous roots and Spanish influence has created a unique culture that can still be felt today in the traditions, customs and mentality of the people. The colonial remains, whether in architecture or stories, are a window into the past and remind us of how a country's history is shaped over time.

Independence and the Emergence of the Republic

The period of independence and the emergence of the Republic of Costa Rica mark a decisive period in the country's history. This period was marked by political upheaval, efforts for sovereignty and the shaping of a new political order. During the colonial period, the seeds of the idea of independence were sown, and during the 19th century, Costa Rica began to forge its own path to becoming an independent nation.

The process of independence from Spain began in the early 19th century and reached Costa Rica in 1821. October 29, 1821 is a key date in the country's history, as it broke away from Spanish colonial rule along with other Central American countries. Costa Rica initially joined the Central American Confederation, a short-lived alliance of Central American states.

The early years after independence were marked by political turbulence and uncertainty. Costa Rica was affected by political instability and internal conflicts that led to a departure from the Central American Confederation. In 1848, Costa Rica finally gained its full sovereignty and declared itself an independent republic. The transition to the republic led to a new political and social order. Constitutions and institutions were created that laid the foundations for the democratic system that continues to shape Costa Rica today. The recognition of individual freedoms and the emphasis on civil rights formed the foundation for the young nation.

A significant milestone in this period was the abolition of the army in 1949. This decision set Costa Rica on a unique course of peace and demilitarization that set the country apart from many other Latin American nations. The decision to invest the financial resources instead in education, health care and social programs resulted in a stable and prosperous society.

Political stability and the emphasis on education led to relative prosperity and a high level of education in Costa Rica. These factors helped Costa Rica become a major player in the international community and establish itself as a pioneer in education, environmental protection, and human rights.

The period of independence and the emergence of the Republic of Costa Rica were marked by ups and downs that shaped the country into what it is today. The efforts for sovereignty, the emergence of democratic institutions and the renunciation of an army have made Costa Rica a unique and admirable country that plays a significant role on the international stage.

Modern History: Progress and Political Development

The modern history of Costa Rica is marked by remarkable progress in various fields and continuous political development. After the turbulent times of independence and the emergence of the republic, Costa Rica began to establish itself as a stable democracy and set itself up for a future of prosperity and social progress.

The 20th century brought important political developments that influenced the direction of the country. In the early decades of the century, Costa Rica pursued an active foreign policy and maintained close relations with the United States. This close cooperation was particularly noticeable during the Cold War period, when Costa Rica received political and economic support from the United States.

One of the most notable developments in Costa Rica's modern history has been the progressive development of the education system. In the 1940s, educational reforms began to make education more accessible to all. The emphasis on education led to an increase in literacy rates and created a well-educated population that would play an important role in the country's economic development.

In the 1980s, Costa Rica also hosted peace negotiations in the region, which led to a solution to the conflict in Nicaragua. This diplomatic role underscored Costa Rica's political stability and commitment to peace and conflict resolution.

Costa Rica's economy experienced diversification and continuous growth throughout the 20th century. While the export of coffee continued to play an important role, other sectors such as tourism, electronics production, and the service industry began to develop. The promotion of the tourism sector through the creation of nature reserves and the emphasis on ecotourism helped make Costa Rica a popular tourist destination.

Costa Rica's political development has been characterized by a strong emphasis on democracy and human rights. The country had free and fair elections, which were held regularly, and a strong civil society that stood up for citizens' rights. Costa Rica had a long tradition of freedom of expression and freedom of the press, which shaped the country's democratic landscape.

Costa Rica's modern history has been marked by progressive political stability, economic growth, and social progress. The emphasis on education, the promotion of tourism, and the commitment to peace and diplomacy have made the country a prominent player in the region and on the international stage. Costa Rica's political development reflects the country's commitment to democracy, human rights and progress.

The rich diversity of fauna and flora

Costa Rica is undoubtedly a jewel of biodiversity and is home to an amazing variety of plants and animals. This rich biodiversity is the result of the country's diverse ecosystems, from the rainforests to the coasts, the mountains and the wetlands. The unique geographical location between North and South America, as well as the different altitudes, have led to Costa Rica becoming a hotspot of biodiversity.

The rainforests of Costa Rica are a true treasure of biodiversity. They are home to an incredible number of plant species, from mighty trees to tiny orchids. The Monteverde Cloud Forest and Corcovado National Park are just two examples of the rich flora found in these habitats. Epiphytes, mosses and ferns are at home in the treetops and create a multi-layered ecosystem.

The wildlife in Costa Rica is just as impressive as the plant life. The rainforest is the habitat for a wide variety of animal species, including various species of monkeys such as howler monkeys, capuchin monkeys, and titi monkeys. Sloths hang leisurely in the trees, while the colorfulness of toucans, hummingbirds and macaws breaks through the sky above the rainforest roof. Anteaters, ocelots and cougars are just a few of the fascinating predators that call the deep forests home.

The coastal areas of Costa Rica are also of great importance for biodiversity. The coastal regions, including the Caribbean coast and the Pacific coast, are breeding grounds for various species of sea turtles. Both the endangered leatherback and the green sea turtles use the beaches to lay their eggs. The coral reefs are home to an abundance of marine life, including colorful fish, sharks, rays, and manta rays.

Costa Rica has also established protected areas and national parks to preserve the amazing biodiversity. Tortuguero National Park on the Caribbean coast is one of the most important turtle sanctiaries in the region. Manuel Antonio National Park offers a unique combination of rainforest and coastline and is known for its biodiversity.

The rich diversity of Costa Rica's fauna and flora attracts tourists, scientists, and nature lovers from all over the world. The treasures of biodiversity that can be found in the country's various ecosystems illustrate the importance of preserving this unique nature. The conservation efforts and the focus on sustainable tourism help to ensure that the splendor of Costa Rica's flora and fauna is preserved for generations to come.

Conservation in Costa Rica: A Pioneer in Environmental Protection

Costa Rica has made a name for itself worldwide as a pioneer in the field of environmental protection and sustainability. The country's rich biodiversity, unique geographical location, and awareness of the importance of conservation have led Costa Rica to become an outstanding example of protecting the environment and biodiversity.

Early on, Costa Rica recognized the need to protect its natural resources. As early as the 1980s, large parts of the country were declared protected areas and national parks. These protected areas encompass various ecosystems, from rainforests to mangrove forests and wetlands. The establishment of such protected areas helped to conserve endangered species and preserve natural habitats.

A notable example of Costa Rica's commitment to conservation is Corcovado National Park. Considered one of the most biodiverse places in the world, this park is home to an incredible variety of plants and animals, including many endemic species. The creation of protected areas such as Corcovado National Park has made it possible to provide a safe habitat for endangered species such as the jaguars, tapirs and the harpy eagle.

Another important initiative is the protection of sea turtles. Costa Rica's beaches are breeding grounds for several species of sea turtles, but they are endangered due to habitat loss and human activities. By protecting nesting sites, monitoring nests, and educating communities, Costa Rica has been able to help stabilize the sea turtle population.

Costa Rica also relies on sustainable tourism to protect the environment. The focus on ecotourism aims to preserve the country's natural treasures while providing visitors with unique and authentic experiences. The development of sustainable tourism practices that respect the environment and engage local communities has made Costa Rica a popular destination for nature lovers.

The Costa Rican government has taken various measures to promote environmental protection. It has enacted environmental laws that limit deforestation, guarantee the protection of flora and fauna and promote sustainable agriculture. The country has also implemented renewable energy programs to reduce its environmental footprint.

Costa Rica's successes in conservation have put it on the world map of environmental protection. The country has proven that economic progress and environmental protection can go hand in hand. Costa Rica's commitment to conservation is an inspiring example of how a nation can make a positive impact on the environment through conscious action and political action.

From coffee plantations to sustainable agriculture

Agriculture has played an important role in Costa Rica's history, shaping the country's economic, social, and cultural fabric. From the early days of coffee plantations to today's emphasis on sustainable practices, Costa Rica's agriculture has continued to evolve and adapt. The era of coffee plantations was a turning point in Costa Rica's agriculture and shaped the country's economic development. In the 19th century, coffee became one of the country's most important exports, creating wealth for many farmers. Coffee cultivation areas stretched across the country's hills and mountainsides, and coffee production was a major contributor to economic development.

However, the focus on coffee cultivation also led to environmental impacts such as deforestation and soil erosion. In the late 20th century, Costa Rica began to recognize the negative consequences of this intensive agriculture and to become more committed to sustainable practices. Promoting agroforestry, where trees are grown along with other crops, helped protect the soil and promote biodiversity. Another focus in sustainable agriculture is organic farming. Many farmers in

Costa Rica have switched to organic farming methods to reduce the use of chemicals and maintain soil health. Organic farming also promotes the preservation of biodiversity and the protection of natural resources. In addition to traditional agricultural practices, Costa Rica has also developed new approaches to sustainable land use. The country has set itself the goal of becoming carbon neutral by 2021 and promoting renewable energy sources. This focus on environmental protection and sustainability is also reflected in agricultural projects that minimize environmental impact and reduce dependence on fossil fuels.

Sustainable agriculture in Costa Rica has a positive impact on communities and the economy. Smallholder farmers play an important role in this movement and contribute to food security. Local markets and community initiatives promote the exchange of knowledge and resources to disseminate sustainable agricultural practices. The journey of coffee plantations to sustainable agriculture illustrates the transformation and adaptability of Costa Rica's agriculture. The emphasis on environmental protection, biodiversity and social responsibility has made the country a model for sustainable development. Agricultural practices in Costa Rica are in line with the desire to conserve natural resources and create a livable future for generations to come.

The variety of delicious Costa Rican cuisine

Costa Rican cuisine is an intriguing blend of local traditions, fresh ingredients, and cultural influences. With its rich agricultural diversity and proximity to the sea, Costa Rica offers a range of delicious dishes that will tantalize the taste buds. From savoury dishes to exotic fruits, Costa Rican cuisine is a real treat for the palate.

The richness of Costa Rican cuisine is reflected in the traditional dishes. The "casado" is a well-known dish that includes a colorful mix of rice, beans, meat or fish, vegetables, plantains and often a fried egg. This dish reflects the culinary diversity of the country and offers a balanced combination of flavors.

The "Gallo Pinto" is another characteristic Costa Rican dish made with rice and beans. It is often served for breakfast and can be supplemented with eggs, meat or creamy sauce. The combination of rice and beans is a foundation of many Costa Rican meals, giving them a unique flavor.

Seafood plays an important role in Costa Rican cuisine, thanks to its coastal location on the Pacific and Caribbean Seas. "Ceviche" is a popular dish of raw fish or seafood, marinated in lime juice and spices. It's refreshing, light, and a favorite among locals and visitors alike.

Costa Rican cuisine is also characterized by its exotic fruits. Fresh pineapples, mangoes, guavas, papayas, and passion fruit are plentiful and are often made into juices, smoothies, or desserts. "Chiverre" is a local type of pumpkin that is made into sweet delicacies such as compote or jam.

A unique culinary experience in Costa Rica is the use of "salsa lizano", a spicy sauce that is added to many dishes. This sauce adds a special touch to food and is an indispensable part of Costa Rican cuisine.

Costa Rican cuisine celebrates not only taste, but also community. Sharing meals with family and friends is an important social tradition. Street markets offer fresh produce and regional specialties that connect with culture and people.

The variety of delicious Costa Rican cuisine is a reflection of the country's cultural riches. The mix of traditional dishes, fresh ingredients and local influences makes Costa Rican cuisine a true voyage of discovery for the palate. Whether you're looking for savory dishes or fruity treats, Costa Rican cuisine invites you to experience the essence of the country in a delicious way.

The magic of traditional dishes

The traditional dishes of Costa Rica are like a culinary window into the history, culture and soul of the country. These dishes have been handed down from generation to generation and reflect people's attachment to their land and identity. Every bite of this delicious food tells a story and reveals the magic that lies within the simple yet flavor-rich flavors.

A highlight of traditional Costa Rican cuisine is the "Gallo Pinto", a dish made from rice and beans. This dish has a long history and is an integral part of the daily life of many Costa Ricans. With its simple preparation and yet delicious flavors, the "Gallo Pinto" symbolizes the down-to-earthness and communal feeling rooted in Costa Rican culture.

Another traditional dish that reflects Costa Rican identity is the "olla de carne". This hearty soup consists of various types of meat, root vegetables and plantains. It is often prepared for special occasions and festivals and brings family and friends together. The "Olla de Carne" is not only a delight for the palate, but also an expression of community and togetherness.

The "Caldillo de Vigilia" is a traditional dish served during Lent. This spicy fish soup symbolizes the religious traditions and beliefs of the people of Costa Rica. Made up of fish, vegetables, and spices, it is an example of the way food is associated with meaning and values in Costa Rican culture.

The "tamales" are another traditional dish that is often prepared on special occasions such as Christmas. They consist of dough filled with meat, vegetables and spices and wrapped in banana leaves. The preparation of "tamales" is often a collaborative project where family members come together to make this special delicacy.

Costa Rican cuisine also reflects the country's close relationship with nature. Fresh ingredients such as tropical fruits, fresh vegetables, fish and seafood play a central role in the traditional dishes. Costa Rican cuisine honors the country's rich biodiversity and celebrates the treasures that nature offers.

The magic of Costa Rica's traditional dishes lies not only in the taste, but also in the stories and values they embody. These dishes are more than just food; they are an expression of history, community and culture. Each bite opens a window into the Costa Rican way of life and reveals the magic hidden in the simple yet meaningful flavors.

Exotic fruits and their meaning

Exotic fruits are a treasure of nature that is present in abundance in Costa Rica. These delicious and diverse fruits are not only a treat for the palate, but also have a profound cultural and environmental significance. From succulent tropical fruits to unique native species, exotic fruits are an important part of the Costa Rican lifestyle.

The banana, one of the most famous exotic fruits, has a long history in Costa Rica. The country is one of the largest banana exporters in the world and has established itself as a major player in the banana industry. The banana plantations shape the landscape and the economy of many communities. However, they are also linked to social and environmental issues that promote awareness of sustainable cultivation and fair working conditions.

The pineapple, another famous tropical fruit, is a symbol of the freshness and diversity of Costa Rican cuisine. The pineapple-growing regions reflect the country's different climates, from the hot coastal areas to the cooler highland regions. However, the pineapple industry also has challenges in terms of resource use and environmental impact, leading to discussions about sustainability.

Mango, papaya, guava, passion fruit, and star fruit are just a few examples of the exotic fruits that thrive in Costa Rica. These fruits are not only delicious, but also rich in vitamins, minerals and antioxidants. They play an important role in the diet of the Costa Rican population and contribute to a healthy lifestyle.

Native fruits such as the "guanábana" or soursop are also of great importance. The guanábana fruit is appreciated for its sweet and sour taste and is often made into drinks, ice cream and desserts. In traditional medicine, it is also used for its presumed health benefits.

Costa Rican culture celebrates exotic fruits not only as food, but also as part of festivals and celebrations. Fruits such as the "carambola" or star fruit are often cut into elaborate decorations and presented as visual highlights on festive tables. This aesthetic recognition of the exotic fruits shows their cultural significance and their role in social gatherings.

The importance of exotic fruits also extends to the tourism sector. Ecotourism and visiting orchards are popular with visitors who take the opportunity to experience the variety of fruits up close. Guided tours of orchards offer insights not only into cultivation and harvesting, but also into sustainability efforts and ecological practices.

Exotic fruits are not only a treat for the palate, but also a reflection of Costa Rica's nature, culture, and social dynamics. They represent the connection between man and nature, between tradition and innovation. From banana to soursop, exotic fruits contribute to a rich culinary experience, reflecting the diversity and beauty of the country.

The fascinating wildlife of Costa Rica

Costa Rica's wildlife is as diverse and fascinating as the country's landscapes themselves. From the dense rainforests to the coastal regions and the highlands, Costa Rica is home to an astonishing biodiversity that impresses nature lovers and researchers alike. Costa Rica's unique geographical location as a link between North and South America has led to it becoming a biodiversity hotspot.

The country's dense rainforests are home to an impressive variety of animal species. Monkeys, including capuchin monkeys, howler monkeys, and titi's monkeys, can be seen in the treetops, while sloths hang leisurely from the branches. The colorful splendor of birds such as toucans, macaws and hummingbirds fascinates viewers. Reptiles such as iguanas, anole lizards and snakes are also part of the rich ecosystem.

The coastal regions of Costa Rica offer a richly laid table for marine life. Both the Caribbean and Pacific coasts are breeding grounds for sea turtles, including the endangered leatherback and the green sea turtle. The coral reefs in the Caribbean are teeming with colorful fish, rays, and other marine life. Whales, dolphins and shark species can be spotted off the Pacific coast.

The forests and mountains of the highlands also provide a habitat for fascinating animal species. The quetzal, a colorful bird with magnificent tail plumage, is a symbol of Costa Rican wildlife and a sought-after photo opportunity for birdwatchers. Tapirs, ocelots and cougars are some of the mammals that are native to the protective forests.

Arenal Volcano National Park is home to a variety of animals, including the famous sloths and the rare jaguars. Manuel Antonio National Park on the Pacific coast is known for its variety of monkey species, including capuchin monkeys and howler monkeys. Corcovado National Park in the south of the country is considered one of the most biodiverse places in the world and is home to a wide variety of plant and animal species.

Costa Rica has also established protected areas and conservation projects to conserve wildlife. These efforts have led to the rescue of endangered species such as the scarlet macaw, a beautiful parrot that was on the verge of extinction. The Costa Rican government has also enacted laws that ensure the protection of endangered species and their habitats.

Costa Rica's fascinating wildlife offers not only visual delights, but also important insights into ecology and conservation. The country's diverse habitats, from the rainforests to the coasts, offer a wealth of opportunities for wildlife viewing and research. The preservation of this amazing wildlife is not only of ecological importance, but also contributes to the creation of a unique and memorable experience for visitors and locals alike.

Rainforest Adventure: On the Trail of Wild Animals

A rainforest adventure in Costa Rica promises an unforgettable journey into a world full of wonders and secrets. The country's lush rainforests are home to an incredible variety of wildlife, from majestic birds to elusive mammals. Such an adventure offers not only the opportunity to experience the fascinating wildlife, but also a deeper understanding of conservation and the importance of preserving these unique ecosystems.

A highlight of any rainforest adventure in Costa Rica is undoubtedly bird watching. The country is home to more than 900 species of birds, including exotic species such as the magnificent quetzal and the colorful toucan. The early hours of the morning are the best time to experience the cheerful chirping and colorful feathers of the birds as the rainforest comes to life.

The nocturnal wildlife of the rainforest is equally exciting. Guided night walks offer the opportunity to spot nocturnal creatures such as bats, moths and frogs. The sounds of the nocturnal rainforest symphony, from calling owls to chirping crickets, create a magical atmosphere that inspires the senses.

The treetops of the rainforest are home to species of monkeys such as capuchin monkeys, howler monkeys and titi monkeys. The curious and playful monkeys are often easy to spot as they swing through the trees and show off their social interactions. A fascinating sight is to observe the monkeys in their natural environment and study their behaviors.

The rainforests of Costa Rica are also the habitat for a variety of reptiles and amphibians. Colorful frogs, which protect themselves from predators by wearing poisonous colors, are particularly impressive. Snake species such as the boa constrictor and the lance viper are also part of the rainforest ecosystem.

One of the most sought-after encounters in a rainforest adventure is the sighting of wild mammals. Ocelots, jaguars, tapirs, and anteaters are some of the elusive and hard-to-spot species. Experienced guides can identify tracks and clues about these animals and help you experience the fascination of tracing their tracks.

The rainforest offers not only opportunities for wildlife viewing, but also insights into the ecological importance of these habitats. The plants, animals and microorganisms interact in complex interactions that maintain the balance of the ecosystem. A rainforest adventure offers the opportunity to learn more about these connections and appreciate the value of conservation.

The rainforests of Costa Rica are places of wonder, discovery and respect for nature. The opportunity to walk in the footsteps of wildlife allows visitors to connect with wildlife and appreciate the beauty and importance of these habitats. A rainforest adventure in Costa Rica is not only a journey into nature, but also a journey to oneself and a deeper understanding of the world around us.

Explore the spectacular variety of birds

Costa Rica's bird diversity is a treasure that attracts avid birdwatchers from all over the world. Over 900 species of birds can be spotted in the country's lush rainforests, mountainous highland regions, and coastal areas. The abundant wildlife ranges from majestic birds of prey to tiny hummingbirds and colorful parrots that fill the sky with colors and songs.

The rainforests are an Eldorado for birdwatchers. Here you can find species such as the quetzal, one of the most magnificent birds in Latin America. Its bright green plumage and long tail make it a sought-after photo opportunity. The quetzal is not only a symbol of natural beauty, but also of the preservation of the rainforests and their habitat.

Many species of birds in Costa Rica are endemic, which means that they are only found in this region. The mangrove flycatcher and the cabanis saltman are examples of such unique species. Being able to observe these rare birds is a special privilege for birdwatchers and helps protect their habitats.

The coastal areas of Costa Rica are a haven for seabirds. Frigatebirds, gannets and pelicans nest on the cliffs of the Pacific coast, while the mangrove forests of the Caribbean coast provide refuges for herons, storks and other waterfowl and waders. Boat trips to the coastal areas allow visitors to experience an impressive variety of seabirds up close.

Hummingbirds are another highlight of Costa Rica's birdlife. These tiny birds with dazzling colors and fast flight maneuvers are a feast for the eyes. The different species of hummingbirds, including the Violet Sabrewing and the Green Violet-throated Hummingbird, fascinate with their elegant movements and unique characteristics.

Birdwatching in Costa Rica is not only a visual experience, but also an acoustic one. The singing of birds fills the air with a natural symphony that varies depending on the time of day and location. The call of the toucan, the song of the bush bunting and the chirping of the warblers are just a few examples of the melodic sounds that fill the rainforest.

The Costa Rican government has been committed to nature conservation and the preservation of bird diversity. Numerous national parks and protected areas provide safe refuges for birds and other animals. One example is Palo Verde National Park, which is known for its large populations of waterfowl that reside in the wetlands and lagoons.

Birdwatching in Costa Rica is more than just a hobby; it is a way to appreciate the beauty of nature and to work for the preservation of the environment. The country's spectacular bird diversity reflects the diversity of ecosystems and emphasizes the need to protect these fragile habitats. A birding adventure in Costa Rica opens your eyes to the wonders of nature and leaves a profound connection with the country's feathered inhabitants.

The Majestic Marine Life: Underwater Paradises

The waters around Costa Rica are rich in breathtaking beauty and fascinating diversity, not only on land but also underwater. The country's underwater paradises offer a unique opportunity to discover the majestic marine life and immerse yourself in a world as impressive as the lush rainforests and diverse landscapes above sea level.

Costa Rica is a true paradise for divers and snorkelers. The waters are home to an astonishing variety of marine life, from colorful corals and tiny fish to majestic whales and mighty sharks. The country's dive sites offer unparalleled opportunities to get up close and personal with the underwater world and admire its beauty.

The coral reefs off the coast of Costa Rica are a treasure trove of biodiversity. They are home to a variety of coral species that form a colorful underwater landscape and provide habitat for countless species of fish. Diving or snorkeling along these reefs is like diving into a colorful painting animated by anemones, starfish, and tropical fish. One of the most impressive phenomena in Costa Rica's waters is the arrival of humpback whales. These majestic sea creatures migrate thousands of kilometers each year to reach the warm waters off the coast of Costa Rica. This is where they give birth to their young, offering visitors a unique spectacle of jumps and tail beats. However, whales are only one part of Costa Rica's diverse marine fauna. Dolphins gliding elegantly alongside boats amaze viewers. Sea turtles, including the endangered leatherback and green sea turtles, nest on the beaches and swim through the waves. Rays, manta rays and various species of sharks are also part of the underwater world.

Costa Rica is committed to protecting marine life and its habitats. Numerous marine protected areas and conservation projects have been established to preserve the fragile ecosystems. These efforts help to preserve biodiversity and promote the sustainable use of marine resources.

The experience of snorkeling and diving in the waters of Costa Rica opens up a new dimension of beauty and wonder. The majestic marine life that lives in the depths of the oceans enchants the senses and leaves unforgettable impressions. The country's underwater paradises invite you to immerse yourself in the world of corals, fish and marine mammals and discover the wonders of the sea, which are as impressive as the treasures on land.

In the footsteps of indigenous cultures

Costa Rica's indigenous cultures are a fascinating insight into the country's historical and cultural diversity. Before the arrival of European settlers, the area that is now Costa Rica was inhabited by various indigenous peoples who maintained their own unique traditions, languages, and ways of life. Exploring this rich history allows us to better understand the roots of Costa Rican culture and promote respect for the diversity of indigenous communities.

The ancestors of today's indigenous population of Costa Rica were closely connected to nature and the land. They made a living from agriculture, fishing and hunting, and had a deep knowledge of the natural resources and medicinal plants of the region. Their traditional practices and beliefs reflected their respect for nature and their dependence on it.

The Bribrí, Cabécar, Boruca, Ngäbe and other indigenous peoples have preserved their own languages, cultural customs and crafts. The traditional handicrafts, including hand-woven fabrics, ornate masks and ceramics, are an expression of their cultural identity and history. These artworks tell stories of mythology, community, and nature.

Festivals and rituals play an important role in the life of Costa Rica's indigenous communities. These events are often closely linked to agriculture, harvesting and the cycle of nature. For example, every year the Boruca celebrate the "Festival de los Diablitos", where they express their history and fighting spirit through colorful masks and dances.

The relationship of indigenous peoples with their land is deeply rooted and has been put to the test throughout history. Traditionally, they have shared and managed the land, with a focus on sustainability and respect for resources. In recent decades, indigenous communities have increasingly fought for their land rights to protect their culture and way of life.

The protection of indigenous cultures and their rights is of great importance in Costa Rica. The country's constitution recognises cultural diversity and protects the rights of indigenous people to land use and self-determination. Government programs and NGOs work to empower indigenous communities and preserve their cultural identity.

Experiencing and respecting Costa Rica's indigenous cultures provides an opportunity to look beyond one's cultural horizons and understand the importance of preserving diversity. Indigenous communities are guardians of knowledge, traditions and sustainable lifestyles that are valuable to society as a whole. Following in the footsteps of indigenous cultures allows us to gain deep insights into Costa Rica's past and present, and to appreciate its rich palette of cultural treasures.

Handicrafts and folk art

Costa Rica's handicrafts and folk art are a reflection of the country's cultural diversity and rich history. These art forms are an expression of the creativity and skill of local artisans who use traditional techniques and materials to create unique works of art. The variety of artisan products reflects the different regions, ethnic groups, and cultural influences that have shaped Costa Rica's rich art scene.

The production of handicrafts in Costa Rica has deep roots in the country's indigenous cultures. From hand-woven textiles and intricately carved wooden figurines to intricately crafted ceramics, each piece reflects the history and traditions of the communities that created it. The use of natural materials such as wood, clay, fabrics and seeds gives each work of art a special authenticity.

A notable form of handicrafts in Costa Rica is the traditional masks. The Boruca community is known for its elaborate masks used during the "Festival de los Diablitos". Not only are these masks intricately carved and painted, but they also carry stories of mythology, tradition, and social expression.

Costa Rica's handicrafts also extend to handmade jewelry. Seeds, stones, and metals are made into unique pieces of jewelry that bear traditional symbols and patterns. These pieces of jewelry are not only ornate accessories, but also carry cultural significance and narratives.

The art of carving is widespread and diverse in Costa Rica. Wood carvings can include religious figures, animals, plants, and abstract designs. The pieces are often painted with natural colors to emphasize their beauty and uniqueness.

Modern artisans in Costa Rica often combine traditional techniques with contemporary designs. This has resulted in a variety of products, including bags, clothing, decorative items, and more, that combine traditional art with modern trends.

Costa Rica's artisan markets and festivals are an excellent way to discover and experience this unique art form. Cities such as San José, Heredia and Sarchí are well-known centers for handicrafts, where visitors can purchase works of art directly from the artisans.

Costa Rica's handicrafts and folk art are not only an expression of creativity, but also a way to preserve the country's cultural identity. These art forms reflect the stories, values, and traditions of the people who created them, contributing to Costa Rica's cultural diversity and heritage. A visit to the craft markets and discovering the handicrafts are a window into the soul of the country and offer a unique opportunity to immerse yourself in the local culture.

Religion and Spirituality in Costa Rica

Costa Rica's religious and spiritual landscape is characterized by a fascinating diversity of faiths that reflect the cultural and historical development of the country. From traditional indigenous practices to the influences of Christianity and other religions, there is a rich mix of beliefs and customs that accompany the people of Costa Rica in their everyday lives.

The indigenous cultures that inhabited the land before the arrival of the Spaniards had their own spiritual beliefs and rituals that were strongly linked to nature. These beliefs have often been passed down through generations in the form of offerings, ceremonies, and stories. Although the influence of Christianity has grown greatly over time, many indigenous customs and beliefs have survived to this day.

With the arrival of the Spaniards in the 16th century, Christianity brought a new religious dimension to Costa Rica. The majority of the Costa Rican population today belongs to the Roman Catholic faith, and churches and cathedrals are important religious and cultural centers in the country. Celebrations on religious occasions, such as Easter and Christmas, are celebrated with special devotion and a sense of community.

In addition to Christianity, Costa Rica is home to a growing number of other religious communities. Protestant churches, including evangelical and Pentecostal churches, have gained influence. Jewish, Buddhist and Muslim communities are also represented in the country, often in smaller numbers, but still part of the diverse religious fabric.

Spirituality plays a significant role in the daily lives of many people in Costa Rica. The close connection to nature and the recognition of natural rhythms are often reflected in spiritual beliefs and practices. An example of this is the belief in "Santos y Santos" (saints and saints), a form of folk religion that combines the veneration of saints with indigenous and African influences.

The spiritual connection with nature is also underlined by the numerous sacred places and sacred springs in the country. Many of these places are visited by believers to ask for health, happiness and blessings. These spiritual places are not only religious sites, but also symbols of the close connection between people and the environment.

Religion and spirituality in Costa Rica reflect the diversity and openness of society. People of different beliefs live peacefully side by side and share a common appreciation for faith, spirituality and traditions. This colorful palette of religious practices and beliefs is a fascinating feature of Costa Rican culture and demonstrates the country's openness to different expressions of spirituality.

Traditional festivals and celebrations

Costa Rica's traditional festivals and celebrations are a reflection of the country's rich cultural history and the diversity of its people. From colorful parades to religious ceremonies, these festivities reflect the identity and values of Costa Rican society.

One of the most famous festivals in Costa Rica is the celebration of the "Dia de la Independencia" on September 15th. This day celebrates Costa Rica's independence from Spain in 1821. The streets are decorated with flags, flowers, and patriotic decorations, and parades, musical performances, and cultural events take place. The celebrations express pride in the country's history and national identity.

Semana Santa, or Holy Week, is an important religious celebration in Costa Rica. In the days leading up to Easter, processions and religious ceremonies take place in which the sufferings and resurrection of Christ are recreated. This time is also an opportunity for many families to gather and pray together.

Another notable festival is the "Festival de los Diablitos" of the Boruca community. This traditional festival tells the story of the struggle of the Boruca against the Spanish conquistadors. Using intricately carved masks and colorful costumes, locals re-enact the battles and events that have played an important role in their people's history.

The "Fiestas Patronales" are local patron saint festivals that are celebrated in various towns and villages. These festivals are a mixture of religious and secular celebrations, with processions, music, dancing and gastronomic events taking precedence. Each community celebrates its patron saint with its own customs and traditions.

The "Carnaval" is an exuberant festival that is celebrated in many cities in Costa Rica. With colorful costumes, music, parades and street parties, the Carnaval marks the beginning of Lent before Easter. It's a time of celebration, joy and exuberance, where people leave their worries behind for a moment.

The "Tope Nacional" is a spectacular horse parade that takes place every year on December 26 in San José. Hundreds of riders proudly display their decorated horses and traditional horsemanship. The event is a tribute to Costa Rica's equestrian culture and agricultural tradition.

The festivals and celebrations in Costa Rica are an integral part of social and cultural life. They offer opportunities for community, cohesion and cultural exchange. These traditional events are not only an opportunity to celebrate, but also a way to get to know the history, culture and people of the country better.

San José: The Vibrant Capital

The capital of Costa Rica, San José, is a fascinating center of culture, history, and urban life. As the political, economic and cultural heart of the country, San José plays a crucial role in Costa Rica's development and identity. This vibrant metropolis attracts visitors with its rich cultural heritage, diverse attractions, and vibrant ambiance.

San José was founded in 1737 and has since grown into a modern city with a storied past. The city's architecture reflects this development, from colonial buildings to modern high-rises. A visit to the historic city center allows visitors to admire the charming colonial architecture and feel the atmosphere of yesteryear.

The city is home to an impressive array of museums that showcase the country's cultural heritage and history. The "Museo Nacional de Costa Rica" shows exhibits on pre-Columbian history, the colonial era and the independence movement. The "Museo del Oro Precolombino" is dedicated to the pre-

Columbian gold treasures and works of art of the indigenous people.

Plaza de la Cultura, a central square in San José, is a popular gathering place for locals and visitors alike. Cultural events, concerts and activities take place here. The square is surrounded by historic buildings such as the Teatro Nacional, an impressive neoclassical-style theater.

San José also boasts a vibrant art scene characterized by galleries and art centers. The "Museo de Arte Costarricense" presents Costa Rican artworks from different eras, while modern galleries exhibit contemporary artists from home and abroad. Street art and graffiti are also part of the city's cultural landscape.

The gastronomy in San José is diverse and reflects the cultural influences of the country. From traditional Costa Rican dishes to international delicacies, visitors will find a wide range of dining experiences. Markets such as the "Mercado Central" offer fresh produce, local specialties and handmade handicrafts.

The nightlife in San José is lively and diverse. Bars, restaurants, live music venues and clubs offer entertainment for all tastes. The city is known for its relaxed and friendly atmosphere, which allows visitors to enjoy Costa Rica's urban life to the fullest.

The people of San José are proud of their city and their cultural identity. The capital not only serves as an important political and economic hub, but is also a place where traditions, art, history and modern life merge. San José is the living expression of Costa Rica's development and a fascinating destination to explore and experience.

Cartago: Historical heritage and modern dynamism

The city of Cartago is a rich source of historical significance and modern dynamism in Costa Rica. As one of the oldest cities in the country, Cartago has a fascinating history ranging from pre-Columbian settlements to colonial times and modern times. This city, which was once the capital of Costa Rica, is a place where history, culture, and progress collide.

The history of Cartago dates back to before the arrival of the Spaniards, when the area was inhabited by indigenous peoples. The indigenous people have left traces of their culture, including stone carvings, pottery and settlement structures. With the arrival of the Spaniards, Cartago was founded in 1563 and quickly became an important political and economic center.

During the colonial period, Cartago was the capital of Costa Rica and an important hub of trade and administration. The city has been the scene of significant historical events, including the independence movement from Spain. The historical heritage is reflected in the colonial buildings that have been preserved in the city, including the Basilica of Nuestra Señora de los Ángeles, one of the most important pilgrimage sites in Costa Rica.

However, the city has also experienced setbacks, including volcanic eruptions and earthquakes that led to its relocation as the capital. However, Cartago remained an important center for education and culture, maintaining its historical importance. The city became the seat of the Archdiocese of Costa Rica and is still home to important educational institutions.

Today, Cartago presents itself as a city that combines both its historical past and modern dynamism. Residents are proud of their traditions and cultural heritage, while at the same time living in a developing society. The city is also a center for education, trade, and agricultural activities.

Cartago offers a mix of historical sites, cultural attractions, and modern amenities. The Basilica of Nuestra Señora de los Ángeles annually attracts pilgrims from all over the world who visit the shrine of the "Black Madonna". The surroundings of the city are characterized by picturesque landscapes, including the Irazú Volcano and Lake Orosí.

The city has also evolved in recent times, with a growing range of restaurants, cafes and shops. Residents and visitors can explore the historic city center, visit local craft markets, and enjoy the relaxed atmosphere of Cartago.

Cartago is a place where history, culture and progress blend harmoniously. The city is a living example of Costa Rica's development from its early beginnings to modern times. The people of Cartago proudly contribute to the preservation of the historical heritage and to shaping the future of the city, which is an unforgettable experience for both locals and visitors.

The colorful coastal town of Puerto Limón

Puerto Limón, the capital of the province of Limón on the Caribbean coast of Costa Rica, is a unique and colorful coastal city that combines a rich cultural mix, breathtaking nature and living traditions. As one of the country's most important port cities, Puerto Limón plays a crucial role in the commercial and tourism industries, while also offering a fascinating insight into the culture and history of Costa Rica's Caribbean communities.

The history of Puerto Limón dates back to the time of Spanish colonial rule. The city was founded in the late 19th century by immigrants from Jamaica who came here to work in the banana industry. This cultural influence can still be felt today, especially in the language, music, food and customs of the communities.

Afro-Caribbean culture is a central feature of Puerto Limón. Residents celebrate their roots with colorful parades, music festivals, and dance events. The "Carnaval de Limón" is one of the most famous festivals in the city and attracts thousands of visitors. During

Carnaval, people dance through the streets in colorful costumes and celebrate the cultural diversity of the region.

The beaches of Puerto Limón are famous for their beauty and unique atmosphere. The warm waters of the Caribbean are perfect for swimming, snorkeling and relaxing. Beaches such as Playa Bonita, Playa Cahuita, and Playa Manzanillo provide a stunning backdrop for water sports activities and marine life watching.

Cahuita National Park, located near Puerto Limón, is an important nature reserve that is home to an impressive variety of flora and fauna. Hiking trails lead through lush rainforest and along the coast, where visitors have the chance to spot monkeys, exotic birds, sea turtles, and more.

The port city is also a major port of call for cruise ships exploring Caribbean waters. The cruise passengers will have the opportunity to get to know the city and its surroundings, buy local souvenirs and experience the rich culture.

The cuisine of Puerto Limón reflects the cultural diversity of the city. With influences from the Caribbean, Africa and Latin

America, the cuisine offers a wide range of aromas and flavors. Dishes such as "rice and beans" are a popular traditional dish, while fresh seafood and tropical fruits play an important role in the local cuisine.

Puerto Limón is not only a port city, but also a cultural center that reflects the unique identity of the communities on Costa Rica's Caribbean coast. The colorful buildings, the vibrant music scene, the Caribbean joie de vivre and the breathtaking nature make Puerto Limón an unforgettable destination. Visitors will have the opportunity to experience the diversity of cultures and landscapes and immerse themselves in the authentic atmosphere of the city.

Pura Vida in Puntarenas: beaches and more

The coastal city of Puntarenas, located on the Pacific coast of Costa Rica, embodies the lifestyle of "Pura Vida" in a special way. With its stunning beaches, diverse recreational activities, and laid-back ambiance, Puntarenas is a haven for visitors who want to enjoy the beauty of nature while experiencing the laid-back Costa Rican way of life.

Puntarenas is known for its beautiful beaches, which offer miles of sand, turquoise waters and a variety of water sports. Playa Doña Ana is a popular spot for a refreshing dip in the sea, while Playa Caldera is a hotspot for surfers looking to conquer the waves. The beaches are also perfect for relaxing walks, sunset watching, and beach activities such as beach volleyball.

Paseo de los Turistas is a popular seafront promenade in Puntarenas lined with restaurants, bars, shops, and souvenir stalls. Here, visitors can not only enjoy the local cuisine, but also purchase handmade artwork and souvenirs. The promenade is a popular meeting place for locals and tourists alike.

Puntarenas is also an ideal starting point for boat trips and whale watching tours. The waters off the coast are home to a wide variety of marine life, including whales, dolphins, and colorful fish species. Observing these majestic creatures in their natural environment is an unforgettable experience.

The ferry port of Puntarenas connects the city with the Nicoya Peninsula and other coastal resorts. The ferry rides offer not only convenient transportation, but also scenic views of the sea and surrounding countryside.

In addition to the beaches, Puntarenas also offers cultural attractions for visitors to discover. The "Museo Histórico Marino de Puntarenas" tells the maritime history of the city and displays models of old ships as well as maritime artefacts. The historic church "Iglesia de Nuestra Señora del Carmen" is another cultural gem that reflects the religious significance of the city.

The culinary scene of Puntarenas is characterized by fresh seafood and local specialties. Visitors can sample grilled fish, ceviche, shrimp, and other delicacies inspired by the rich waters of the Pacific. The restaurants along the coast offer not only delicious food, but also spectacular views of the sea.

In Puntarenas, visitors experience the Pura Vida feeling in its purest form. The laid-back way of life, awe-inspiring natural beauty and warm hospitality of the locals make this coastal town an unforgettable destination. Puntarenas offers the perfect blend of adventure, relaxation and cultural experience that makes it a true highlight in Costa Rica.

The historical significance of Heredia

The city of Heredia, also known as "La Ciudad de las Flores" (The City of Flowers), is a gem in Costa Rica that holds a rich history and cultural heritage. Its historical significance spans centuries and has shaped the social, cultural and economic life of the country.

The origins of Heredia date back to the 16th century, when the region was inhabited by indigenous peoples. The city was officially founded in 1706 and quickly developed into an important trading center. In the centuries that followed, Heredia experienced a boom in various fields, including agriculture, education, and handicrafts.

Heredia played an important role in Costa Rica's independence movement from Spanish colonial rule. During this time, courageous citizens gathered in the city to stand up for the country's freedom. The historic "Iglesia de la Inmaculada Concepción" (Church of the Immaculate Conception) was a meeting place for these activities and remains an important historical site to this day. The architecture of Heredia is characterized by colonial buildings and charming squares. Downtown is a maze of cobblestone streets lined with colorful houses. Many of these buildings have historical significance and tell stories of times gone by.

The city is also home to Costa Rica's oldest university, the Universidad Nacional (UNA). This educational institution has a long history and helps shape the educational landscape of the country. The university plays an important role in educating future generations of professionals and researchers. Heredia is also known for its traditional festivals and customs. The "Festival de las Flores" (Flower Festival) is one of the most remarkable events in the city, with colourful parades, flower exhibitions and cultural activities. These festivals are an expression of the proud identity of the city and its inhabitants.

The people of Heredia are proud of their city and its heritage. The city has managed to preserve its historical significance while striving towards a modern future. The locals are committed to preserving cultural traditions while being part of a changing society.

Overall, Heredia embodies Costa Rica's diverse and rich history. The city is a scene of historical events, cultural activities and artistic treasures. Due to its historical importance and its role in the development of the country, Heredia is a city that deserves to be discovered and experienced.

Alajuela: Home of the Arenal Volcano

The city of Alajuela, the second largest city in Costa Rica, is not only a cultural center, but also the starting point for a remarkable natural wonder - the Arenal Volcano. Often referred to as the "Ciudad de los Mangos" (City of Mangoes), the Alajuela region is a place of diversity, adventure and impressive landscapes.

The Arenal Volcano, one of the most active volcanoes in the country, is the most prominent geographical feature of Alajuela. With its symmetrical cone shape and regular eruptions, the Arenal exerts an intriguing attraction on locals and tourists alike. Thought extinct until its last major eruption in 1968, the volcano quickly became a popular destination for nature lovers and adventure seekers.

The surroundings of the Arenal offer a wide range of activities and experiences. Hiking trails lead through the lush rainforest, allowing visitors to discover the region's unique flora and fauna. Arenal National Park is a protected area that is home to a variety of animal and plant species, including monkeys, birds, butterflies, and orchids.

Another highlight near Alajuela is Lake Arenal, which stretches at the foot of the volcano. Not only does the lake offer a picturesque backdrop, but it also offers opportunities for kayaking, fishing, and relaxing. Visitors can enjoy the serene atmosphere of the lake while admiring the majestic presence of the volcano in the background.

The Arenal Hot Springs are another draw for travelers. These natural hot springs offer a relaxing way to unwind after a day of adventure. Many of the nearby resorts have thermal pools and spa facilities that benefit from the beneficial properties of the natural spring water.

The city of Alajuela itself also has a rich history and cultural significance. The historic "Catedral de Alajuela" (Cathedral of Alajuela) is an important religious building and a landmark of the city. The Juan Santamaría Museum honors Costa Rica's national hero and offers insights into the country's history.

Alajuela is also known for its fertile soils and agriculture. The region is an important growing place for coffee, sugar cane, pineapples and, of course, mangoes. The markets of Alajuela offer fresh local produce and are a showcase for the agricultural diversity of the area.

The combination of the picturesque beauty of the Arenal Volcano and the cultural diversity of Alajuela makes this part of Costa Rica an unforgettable destination. Visitors will have the opportunity to experience nature in all its glory, discover the history and culture of the city while enjoying the unique charm of the region.

Cultural diversity of the population

Costa Rica is a country known for its remarkable cultural diversity and ethnic composition. The country's population reflects a fascinating mix of indigenous peoples, African influences, European ancestry, and Asian roots. Over the centuries, this cultural melange has given rise to a unique identity that is reflected in the country's language, art, music, cuisine and traditions.

Costa Rica's indigenous peoples, including the Bribri, Cabécar, Boruca and Ngäbe, contribute significantly to the country's cultural diversity. Their traditional customs, crafts, languages, and spiritual practices are an important part of national identity. The country's government is committed to protecting and promoting the rights and cultural integrity of indigenous peoples.

The African influences come mainly from the Afro-Caribbeans who came to Costa Rica in the 19th century to work in the banana industry. Their music, dance styles such as calypso and traditional festivals such as the

"Carnaval de Limón" are living testimonies to their cultural presence. The Afro-Caribbean community has also influenced Costa Rican cuisine, especially with dishes such as rice and beans and coconut-based dishes.

Costa Rica's European roots date back to the Spanish colonial era. The Spanish language and the Catholic religion have had a profound influence on the country's culture. Traditional festivals such as the "Fiesta de los Diablitos" in Boruca, which represent the struggle between indigenous peoples and the Spaniards, show the fusion of these cultural influences.

Costa Rica's Asian community, mainly of Chinese descent, has also left its mark. Chinese immigrants arrived in the country in the 19th century and have brought their culinary influences to Costa Rican cuisine. Popular dishes such as "chop suey" and "arroz cantonés" are examples of this culinary fusion.

The diversity of cultures in Costa Rica is also reflected in the country's numerous festivals and events. Every year, people celebrate various religious, cultural and historical events with colorful parades, music, dancing and culinary specialties. These festivals are an opportunity to celebrate and appreciate the country's cultural diversity.

Overall, the cultural diversity of Costa Rica's population is a source of pride and identity for the country. The fusion of different traditions and roots has created a unique culture that unites Costa Ricans and makes their country a place of cultural discovery and encounter.

Music and dance: rhythm in the life of the Ticos

Music and dance play a central role in the cultural life of Costa Ricans, also known as "Ticos". From traditional sounds to modern influences, the musical expressions reflect the diversity and vibrant nature of Costa Rican culture. In every corner of the country, there are rhythms that bring people together, tell stories and express emotions.

Costa Rica's traditional music is deeply rooted in the country's cultural roots. Folk music includes styles such as "cumbia", "guaracha" and "tambito", which are often played with guitars, drums and other traditional instruments. These sounds are often accompanied by lively dance steps and are an important part of festivals, celebrations, and other social events.

One of the most characteristic dance styles in Costa Rica is the "Punto Guanacasteco", a traditional couple dance from the province of Guanacaste. Accompanied by guitars and characteristic costumes, the couples dance in rhythmic movements that reflect the joy and life of this region.

Modern music genres such as salsa, reggaeton and hip-hop have also found a large following in Costa Rica. The younger generation has picked up on these musical currents and integrated them into Costa Rican culture. Dance clubs and concerts offer opportunities to experience and enjoy the variety of modern sounds.

An important event in the Costa Rican music world is the "Festival Internacional de las Artes" (International Festival of Arts), which takes place every two years. This festival brings together national and international artists to celebrate music, dance, theatre and visual arts. It is an opportunity to experience the cultural dynamism of the country in all its facets.

The Costa Rican music scene has also produced talented artists who have gained international recognition. Artists such as Manuel Obregón, Editus and Debi Nova are examples of musicians who bring Costa Rican culture to the world.

Dance is not only an artistic form of expression, but also a way to preserve traditions and stories. The "Bailes de los Diablitos" (Dances of the Little Devils) of the Boruca Indians are an example of dances that represent historical events and bring generations of Costa Ricans closer to their cultural identity.

Overall, the music and dance is a vibrant centerpiece of Costa Rican culture. They are means of communication, celebration of identity, and connecting people. Whether traditional or modern, the sounds and rhythms bring the Ticos together, creating a vibrant and dynamic cultural landscape.

Literature and Art Scene in Costa Rica

The literature and art scene in Costa Rica is a fascinating showcase of creativity, expression, and intellectual depth. Both literature and art have a long history and are deeply rooted in the country's cultural identity. From renowned writers to emerging artists, the scene reflects the diversity and richness of Costa Rican culture.

Costa Rica's literary scene has produced numerous notable writers who have gained recognition both nationally and internationally. A prominent figure is the Nobel Prize winner for literature, Gabriel García Márquez, who is considered one of the most influential authors of the 20th century. His work "One Hundred Years of Solitude" has had a lasting impact on the Latin American literary landscape.

Costa Rican literature encompasses a wide range of genres, from poetry to novels to essays and short stories. Authors such as Carmen Lyra, Yolanda Oreamuno and Carlos Luis Fallas have shed light on the country's social and political issues and shaped Costa Rican identity with their works.

The art scene in Costa Rica is just as diverse and dynamic. The visual arts have a long tradition dating back to pre-Columbian times. Indigenous cultures developed artistic techniques such as ceramics and painting, which persist to this day. Modern Costa Rican artists such as Francisco Amighetti and Manuel de la Cruz González have further developed these traditions and created innovative works of art.

The capital, San José, is a hub for art galleries, museums, and cultural events. The "Museo de Arte Costarricense" (Museum of Costa Rican Art) houses an impressive collection of paintings, sculptures and works of art from different eras. The "Teatro Nacional" (National Theatre) is an architectural gem and an important venue for cultural performances.

The literary and art scene in Costa Rica is also a platform for social and political discussions. Artists and writers often advocate for social justice, human rights, and environmental protection. Literary festivals such as the "Festival Internacional de Poesía" (International Poetry Festival) provide a space for the exchange of ideas and the promotion of cultural development.

The younger generation of artists and writers has taken up the legacy of their predecessors and combined it with contemporary approaches. The Costa Rican art and literature scene remains vibrant and changeable, with new voices and perspectives constantly being added.

Overall, Costa Rica's literary and art scene is a vibrant expression of the country's identity, history, and creative energy. It shows the diversity of culture, the voices of the past and the visions of the future. The works of the writers and artists are a window into the soul of Costa Rica and a reflection of what it means to be a "Tico".

Family structures and social norms

Family structures and social norms in Costa Rica are closely intertwined and play a central role in people's lives. Traditional values, modern influences and the diversity of cultures shape the social fabric of the country. Costa Rican society is characterized by strong family ties, gender roles, and respectful relationships.

The family has a high status in Costa Rica and is considered the foundation of society. Multigenerational households are common, with grandparents, parents, and children often living under the same roof. This close family bond fosters cohesion and support within the family.

Gender roles continue to play an important role in Costa Rican society, although changes are also noticeable. Traditionally, men were responsible for providing for the family, while women had the primary responsibility for raising children and running the household. In recent decades, however, gender roles have changed as women enter the workforce and men become more involved in family responsibilities.

Gender equality is an increasing issue in Costa Rica, especially in urban areas. Women have increased access to education and job opportunities, which has led to increased independence and freedom of choice. Nevertheless, there are still cultural and social norms that reflect traditional gender roles.

Respect, courtesy, and family values are of great importance in Costa Rican culture. People value good manners and respectful behavior towards elders and authorities. These values are reflected in everyday interactions, but also in festivals and celebrations.

Religion also plays a role in social norms in Costa Rica. The country is majority Catholic, and religious traditions and values influence daily life. Festivals such as "Semana Santa" (Holy Week) are celebrated intensively by many people and reflect the influence of religion on culture.

Overall, Costa Rica's family structures and social norms reflect the balance between tradition and modernity. The connection to the family, respect for traditions and adaptation to changing social values are characteristics that shape the Costa Rican identity.

Education system and intellectual heritage

Costa Rica's education system has a long history and plays a crucial role in the country's intellectual development. From primary school to university, Costa Rica places a high value on education as the key to personal and social development. The country's intellectual heritage is evident in its educational infrastructure, universities, and commitment to research and innovation.

Costa Rica's education system is free and mandatory for children from 6 to 18 years old. Primary and secondary education is of high quality and has a high enrolment rate. The government has pursued a policy of universal education promotion to ensure that education is accessible to all and that the intellectual potential of the young generation is encouraged.

An important institution in the education system is the "Universidad de Costa Rica" (University of Costa Rica), one of the oldest and most prestigious universities in Latin America. It offers a wide range of degree programs in the humanities, science, engineering, social sciences, and more. The university plays a crucial role in promoting research, science and culture in the country.

The commitment to education and intellectual development is also reflected in the national culture. Costa Rica has a high literacy rate, which contributes to a high level of political participation and civic engagement. People are actively involved in educational initiatives, non-profit organizations, and cultural events that contribute to the intellectual development of the country.

The promotion of research and innovation is another feature of Costa Rica's intellectual heritage. The country is committed to advancing sustainable development, environmental protection, and social justice through research and technology. Institutions such as the "Centro Nacional de Alta Tecnología" (National Center for High Technology) promote scientific research and technological innovation in various fields.

However, the Costa Rican educational landscape also faces challenges. The quality of education can vary depending on the region and socio-economic background. The government is working to reduce these inequalities and ensure equal educational opportunities for all.

Overall, Costa Rica's education system is a key factor in the country's intellectual development and progress. The emphasis on education, research, and cultural participation contributes to Costa Rica's perception as an intellectual center in the region. The educational infrastructure, universities and commitment to intellectual growth are essential elements of the country's cultural heritage.

Language and dialects of indigenous peoples

The diversity of languages and dialects of Costa Rica's indigenous peoples reflects the cultural richness of the country. These languages are not only a means of communication, but also contribute to the preservation of the cultural identity and heritage of indigenous communities. In the midst of change and globalization, indigenous languages have played an important role in maintaining the traditional way of life and passing on knowledge.

Costa Rica is home to eight indigenous groups, each with its own language or dialects. The Bribri, Cabécar, Maleku, Ngäbe, Buglé, Huetar, Chorotega and Teribe are the indigenous peoples who enrich the cultural landscape of the country. Each community has its own language, which not only serves as a means of communication, but also carries deep cultural and spiritual meaning.

The Bribri language is spoken by the Bribri community in the southern part of the country. She is known for her melodic intonation and her close connection to nature.

The Cabécar language, spoken by the Cabécar people of the eastern part of Costa Rica, is rich in words and expressions that reflect the natural environment and the traditional knowledge of the community.

The indigenous languages are crucial for the transmission of stories, legends and traditional knowledge from one generation to the next. They play an important role in rites, ceremonies and cultural events and contribute to strengthening cohesion within communities.

However, the preservation of indigenous languages and dialects is not without its challenges. The spread of Spanish as the dominant language and increasing globalization have meant that some of the indigenous languages are under threat. Young people often grow up speaking Spanish and may have less access to the traditional languages and cultural practices.

In order to protect and promote indigenous languages, both the government and the indigenous communities themselves have taken initiatives. Educational programs, schools, and cultural activities have been developed to preserve indigenous languages and raise awareness of their importance among the younger generation.

Overall, the languages and dialects of indigenous peoples are a valuable treasure in Costa Rica's cultural heritage. Not only do they contribute to the country's diversity, but they are also a reflection of the deep connection between indigenous communities and their environment. The preservation and promotion of these languages are crucial to preserving the cultural identity and heritage of Costa Rica's indigenous peoples.

The Importance of Ecotourism in Costa Rica

Ecotourism has gained exceptional importance in Costa Rica and has become a key industry. The country has built a global reputation as a pioneer in sustainable tourism, combining conservation, cultural appreciation and economic development. Ecotourism in Costa Rica is much more than just an economic activity – it is a philosophy that respects nature while providing travelers with unforgettable experiences.

Costa Rica's rich biodiversity, stunning landscapes, and diverse ecosystems provide the ideal backdrop for ecotourism. From dense rainforests to tropical beaches and volcanic landscapes, the country offers an impressive variety of natural treasures. Ecotourism allows visitors to get up close and personal with these natural wonders while helping to protect them.

One reason for the success of ecotourism in Costa Rica is the careful planning and sustainable development of tourism offerings. Many tour companies work closely with local communities to ensure that income from tourism goes towards environmental conservation and local social projects. The involvement of the local population also promotes awareness of the importance of nature conservation and helps to preserve cultural identity.

National parks and protected areas are at the heart of ecotourism in Costa Rica. These areas offer visitors the opportunity to explore untouched nature and observe rare animal and plant species in their natural habitat. The "Parque Nacional Manuel Antonio" is one of the most famous examples where rainforest and coastal habitats coexist harmoniously. The "Parque Nacional Tortuguero" also attracts thousands of visitors every year to watch the sea turtles lay their eggs.

Ecotourism has not only environmental benefits, but also economic impacts. It contributes to the creation of jobs in rural communities and promotes the local economy. Hotels, restaurants, tour operators, and souvenir shops benefit from the influx of visitors, improving the quality of life of communities.

The Costa Rican government has been actively promoting ecotourism by enacting laws and policies to preserve nature and sustainably develop the tourism sector. The "Certificado para la Sostenibilidad Turística" (Certificate of Sustainable Tourism) is awarded to companies that meet strict sustainability criteria. This promotes accountability and commitment to environmental protection.

Ecotourism in Costa Rica offers a win-win situation for both visitors and the environment. Travelers can experience unforgettable adventures while helping to protect nature and support the local economy. Costa Rica is a shining example of how tourism can contribute to positive change that takes into account both environmental and social aspects.

National Parks and Protected Areas: Preserving Natural Treasures

Costa Rica's national parks and protected areas are true treasures of nature and are at the heart of the effort to preserve the country's unique biodiversity and ecosystems. These protected areas span different regions of the country and offer visitors the opportunity to experience the pristine beauty of nature up close.

Costa Rica has an impressive number of national parks and protected areas that cover more than a quarter of its land area. These areas were established to protect endangered species, preserve habitats, and preserve the country's unique flora and fauna. The "Parque Nacional Corcovado", for example, is known for its high biodiversity and is one of the most ecologically diverse areas in the world.

The diversity of national parks and protected areas reflects Costa Rica's diverse ecosystems. From the dense rainforest of Parque Nacional Braulio Carrillo to the arid savannah of Parque Nacional Santa Rosa, these areas offer a glimpse into the different faces of nature. The rich biodiversity includes monkeys, birds, butterflies, reptiles and a variety of plant species.

An important aspect of national parks and protected areas is the conservation of endangered species. The "Parque Nacional Marino Ballena", for example, is an important refuge for whales and dolphins, which have their migration routes here. The "Parque Nacional Tortuguero" is famous for the laying of eggs by sea turtles on its beaches. These protected areas play a crucial role in the conservation and protection of endangered species.

The Costa Rican government has enacted strict laws and regulations to protect the national parks and protected areas. These laws set out how the areas can be used to ensure that nature and ecosystems remain intact. Entrance fees are collected from visitors to fund conservation and protection efforts.

The national parks and protected areas serve not only to preserve nature, but also to educate and sensitize visitors. Many parks offer guided tours, hiking trails, and informative panels that provide visitors with insight into the area's ecological significance and cultural history. These educational initiatives help to raise awareness of environmental protection.

Overall, the national parks and protected areas are invaluable to Costa Rica. They represent the country's commitment to conservation and offer visitors the opportunity to experience the amazing diversity of nature. These protected areas are not only places of discovery and recreation, but also instruments of environmental protection and sustainable development.

Beaches, Volcanoes and Adventure: Tourism Highlights

Costa Rica is a country of breathtaking beauty and unforgettable adventures, and its beaches, volcanoes, and natural attractions attract millions of visitors annually. The variety of landscapes allows travelers to experience a wide range of activities, from laid-back beach vacations to exciting outdoor adventures.

Costa Rica's coastline stretches for more than 1,290 kilometers and offers an amazing variety of beaches. Whether it's black sand beaches, white sand beaches or secluded coves, there's something for everyone. Playa Manuel Antonio is one of the most popular beaches in the country and is known for its dazzling white sand and crystal clear waters. At the "Playa Tamarindo" water sports enthusiasts will find optimal conditions for surfing.

Costa Rica's volcanoes give the country a unique scenic splendor while offering exciting opportunities for adventure. The "Arenal Volcano" is one of the most active volcanoes in the country and attracts visitors who want to enjoy the hot springs and the surrounding nature. The "Poás Volcano", on the other hand, offers spectacular views of its turquoise crater lake and is a popular destination for nature lovers.

Adventurous visitors will also find what they are looking for in Costa Rica. The "Monteverde Cloud Forest" is a mecca for naturalists and offers a variety of hiking trails and ziplining opportunities. The "Montezuma Falls" are a popular destination for trekking tours and swimming fun. The country also offers rafting adventures on the wild rivers, as well as diving and snorkeling in the clear waters of the Pacific and Caribbean Seas.

The wildlife in Costa Rica is as fascinating as it is diverse. The "Corcovado National Park" is home to an impressive biodiversity, including tapirs, cougars and monkeys. The "Tortuguero National Park" is an important habitat for sea turtles, which lay their eggs here. Birdwatchers will find a rich birdlife in the "Caño Negro Reserve", including the colorful quetzal.

Ecotourism plays an important role in these attractions, as strict rules and regulations help protect the fragile ecosystems. Many of these attractions offer guided tours that convey not only the beauty of nature, but also the importance of protecting the environment.

Costa Rica's beaches, volcanoes, and adventures are at the heart of tourism in this diverse country. They offer visitors unforgettable experiences and opportunities to discover the breathtaking beauty and rich nature of the country. At the same time, great importance is attached to using and protecting these attractions sustainably in order to enable future generations to enjoy the same experiences.

The mysterious cloud forest region of Monteverde

The Monteverde cloud forest region of Costa Rica is a fascinating and mystical environment, characterized by dense fog, lush vegetation, and unique wildlife. This area stretches across the mountains of the Cordillera de Tilarán in the center of the country and attracts nature lovers, adventurers, and explorers alike.

The Monteverde Cloud Forest is characterized by its lush vegetation, characterized by the high humidity and fog. The treetops are covered with epiphytic plants, such as bromeliads and orchids, that thrive in this humid environment. The cloud forest is an important water reservoir for the surrounding areas and helps regulate the flow of water.

This region is also home to an amazing variety of animal species. The famous quetzal, a colorful bird revered as a symbol of freedom and beauty, can be observed here. Rare mammals such as the three-fingered sloth and the ocelot are also inhabitants of this mysterious environment. The biodiversity and endemic animal species make Monteverde a paradise for nature lovers and ornithologists.

One of the main attractions of the Monteverde Cloud Forest is the suspension bridges, which allow visitors to walk through the treetops at lofty heights and get a unique view of the vegetation and wildlife. The "Sky Walk" tour takes you over bridges and platforms laid out between the trees and offers a unique perspective of the cloud forest.

Adventurous travelers can also experience ziplining in Monteverde, which offers an exhilarating way to fly above the treetops and feel the thrill of flying. In addition, the region offers hiking trails for all levels, allowing visitors to experience the beauty of nature up close.

The inhabitants of Monteverde, known as "Ticos", have been actively involved in the preservation of the cloud forest and the promotion of sustainable tourism. The community has a unique relationship with nature and is committed to preserving the ecological integrity of the region.

Overall, the mysterious cloud forest region of Monteverde offers a unique opportunity to experience the beauty of nature in its purest form. The combination of lush vegetation, impressive wildlife, and exciting activities makes this place one of the most remarkable destinations in Costa Rica, transporting visitors to a world of mystery and discovery.

Manuel Antonio: Tropical beauty and biodiversity

A true gem of tropical beauty, the picturesque region of Manuel Antonio on Costa Rica's Pacific coast delights visitors with its stunning scenery, diverse wildlife, and dazzling beaches. This paradise harmoniously combines the elements of the rainforest and the sea, attracting nature lovers, adventurers and recreation seekers alike.

The "Parque Nacional Manuel Antonio" is the heart of this region and one of the most famous national parks in Costa Rica. It encompasses both dense rainforest and pristine beaches that combine to create an impressive backdrop. This park was founded in 1972 and is one of the most popular tourist destinations in the country.

The biodiversity in the "Parque Nacional Manuel Antonio" is impressive. Monkeys, sloths, iguanas, anteaters and numerous species of birds are just some of the animals that can be observed here. Particularly noteworthy is the number of monkey species, including capuchin monkeys and squirrel monkeys, which can often be seen in the treetops.

The beaches of Manuel Antonio are characterized by natural beauty. Playa Espadilla is the most accessible beach in the park and offers fine white sand and turquoise waters. Playa Manuel Antonio, on the other hand, is known for its picturesque sunsets and the opportunity for snorkeling and diving.

The park's rainforest offers hiking trails that take visitors through lush vegetation and biodiverse environments. From the elevated paths, guests can observe exotic plants and animals in their natural habitat. The view from the "Mirador Punta Catedral" offers a breathtaking view of the surrounding coast and the sea.

The conservation of the "Parque Nacional Manuel Antonio" is at the heart of the efforts to protect this unique nature. Visitors are encouraged to abide by the park's rules to preserve the delicate environment. The limited number of visitors per day helps to minimize the ecological footprint.

The Manuel Antonio region offers not only nature experiences, but also a variety of activities for visitors. From kayaking and stand-up paddleboarding to whale-watching tours and canopy tours, there's something for everyone to explore here. The choice of restaurants and accommodation ensures that visitors can enjoy their stay to the fullest.

Manuel Antonio is a place that embodies the true beauty of Costa Rica's tropical nature. The combination of rainforest and coast, the impressive wildlife and the numerous leisure activities make this place an unforgettable destination for all those who want to be enchanted by the fascination of nature.

The fascinating experience of volcanoes

Volcanoes are fascinating natural phenomena that evoke both admiration and respect around the world. Costa Rica is home to an impressive number of volcanoes that not only dot the landscape but also provide a fascinating experience for travelers. These majestic fire-breathers are an important part of the country's geological history and have an unparalleled appeal for adventurers, scientists, and nature lovers.

One of Costa Rica's most prominent volcanoes is the "Arenal Volcano". With its perfectly shaped conical shape, it rises majestically above the surrounding landscape. This volcano was one of the most active volcanoes in the country until its last eruption in 2010, attracting visitors with its impressive lava flows and glowing fountains. Today, the "Arenal" is wrapped in dense vegetation and offers hiking trails that allow visitors to experience the volcanic environment up close. Another impressive volcano is the "Poás Volcano", which is home to the crater lake of the same name. This crater lake is one of the largest in the world and is characterized by its turquoise blue color. Visitors can hike to the crater lake and enjoy the impressive views of the bubbling volcanic lake. The nearby "La Paz Waterfall Gardens" offer an opportunity to discover different waterfalls and animal species.

The "Irazú Volcano" is the highest volcano in Costa Rica and often offers spectacular views of the surrounding landscape due to its height of over 3,400 meters. On a clear day, visitors can enjoy the view over the crater and all the way to the Pacific Ocean. The crater itself is characterized by a lunar landscape that is reminiscent of a pristine, alien world.

Costa Rica's volcanic landscapes offer not only impressive views, but also plenty of activities for the adventurous. In addition to hiking to the peaks of the volcanoes, there are also opportunities for ziplining and mountain biking. Many of the volcanoes are surrounded by national parks, which not only protect nature, but also provide information centers and hiking trails for visitors.

The fascinating world of volcanoes in Costa Rica is an invitation to explore the power of nature and the geological history of the country. From the majestic cones to the crater lakes, these volcanoes offer a variety of experiences that captivate travelers. Being able to get close to an active or extinct volcano and feel the power of the earth makes this experience an unforgettable part of the Costa Rica trip.

The Future of Costa Rica: Challenges and Opportunities

Costa Rica's future faces a host of challenges and opportunities that will influence the country on its path to sustainable development and prosperity. While Costa Rica has already made significant progress in areas such as environmental protection and education, there are still important decisions to be made that will shape the country's fate in the years to come.

One of the biggest challenges is conserving the country's impressive biodiversity and natural resources. Costa Rica has made a name for itself as a pioneer in environmental protection, with an impressive number of national parks and protected areas covering a wide variety of ecosystems. However, the conservation of these natural treasures is an ongoing task that requires continued efforts to curb illegal logging, poaching and pollution.

Another important issue is social justice and reducing inequality in the country. Despite advanced education and health systems, there are still regions and population groups affected by poverty and social disadvantage. The government is working to promote equal opportunities and improve living conditions for all citizens.

The growing tourism sector offers opportunities for economic growth, but also poses challenges in terms of environmental impact and sustainability. Costa Rica is committed to sustainable tourism and implements measures to minimize negative impacts on the environment and engage local communities. However, the right balance between tourism development and nature conservation will continue to be an important task.

The promotion of renewable energies is another key issue for the future of Costa Rica. The country has already made great strides by meeting a significant part of its energy needs from renewable sources such as hydro, wind and solar. Continuing this development will help reduce dependence on fossil fuels and minimize environmental impact.

Education also plays a crucial role in the future development of the country. Costa Rica has a high literacy rate and emphasizes quality education from elementary school to university. Investment in education and research is crucial to nurturing the next generation of professionals and innovators and preserving the country's intellectual heritage.

Costa Rica's future is marked by a dynamic mix of challenges and opportunities. Efforts to protect the environment, social justice, sustainable economic development and education will be instrumental in keeping the country on track. Costa Rica has the opportunity to continue its success story and continue to be a role model for other countries striving for a good balance between prosperity and conservation.

Epilogue

Costa Rica, the land of wonder and diversity, has taken us on a fascinating journey through its history, culture, nature and future prospects. In this book, we explored the country's rich history from indigenous cultures to modern development. We discovered the impressive fauna and flora that shape Costa Rica's ecosystems and admired the country's conservation efforts. We enjoyed the delicious cuisine and understood the importance of ecotourism in preserving the environment.

Costa Rica shows us that it is possible to combine tradition and progress, natural beauty and modern development. The balance between environmental protection and economic prosperity is an example of the country's foresight and commitment, which is a shining inspiration to the world.

The future of Costa Rica will be marked by challenges, whether in environmental protection, social justice or sustainable development. Continuing the country's success story will require the commitment of the government, the people, and the global community to address these challenges.

Costa Rica teaches us that protecting nature and promoting culture can go hand in hand to create a vibrant and sustainable society. The diversity of landscapes and ways of life in Costa Rica reflects how wealth can be defined on many levels.

May this book help to appreciate and celebrate the beauty and importance of Costa Rica. It's an invitation to explore this fascinating land, from the peaks of volcanoes to the beaches of the Pacific, from the lush rainforests to the vibrant cities.

We thank Costa Rica for the privilege of discovering its history and culture. May this book help raise awareness of this unique country and preserve the wonders of Costa Rica for future generations.

Printed in Great Britain
by Amazon